Lamb of Glory

A Musical Service Honoring the Death and Resurrection of Our Lord

by Camp Kirkland

CONTENTS

THE LAMB OF GLORY MEDLEY 2
    Lamb of Glory
    The Lamb
    God Hath Provided the Lamb
IT'S STILL THE CROSS 13
THEY TOOK HIM DOWN (reading) 20
WOUNDED LAMB (underscore) 21
MY REDEEMER LIVES MEDLEY 23
    My Redeemer Lives
    Jesus Has Risen
Artwork 39

The Lamb of Glory

Lamb of Glory
The Lamb
God Hath Provided the Lamb

Arr. by Camp Kirkland

With power ♩ = ca. 70

CD: 1

*"Lamb of Glory" (Nelson/McHugh)

Pre - cious Lamb of glo -

ry, Love's most won - drous sto -

Narrator: In God's eyes He was like a tender green shoot, sprouting from a root in dry and sterile ground.

4

But in our eyes there was no attractiveness at all, nothing to make us want Him. We despised Him and rejected Him– a man of sorrows, acquainted with bitterest grief. Yet it was our grief He bore; our sorrows weighed Him down.

And we thought His troubles were punishment from God for His own sins. We are the ones who strayed away like sheep! Yet God laid on Him the guilt and sins of everyone of us. (Isaiah 53:2, 3a, 4, 6, TLB)

CD: 3

5

6

*"God Hath Provided the Lamb" (Almond)

It's Still the Cross

Words and Music by
NILES BOROP, MIKE HARLAND,
LUKE GARRETT and BUDDY MULLINS
Arr. by Camp Kirkland

judg - ments of the mind._____ It's the op - po - site____ of pol - i - tics,
prove and grant de - grees._____ But the world is out____ there watch - ing, and

Oo_____

pow - er and pres - tige._____ It's a - bout a sim - ple mes - sage and
what they need from us_____ Is to see our ris - en Sav - ior re -

CD: 9   1st time
CD: 11   2nd time

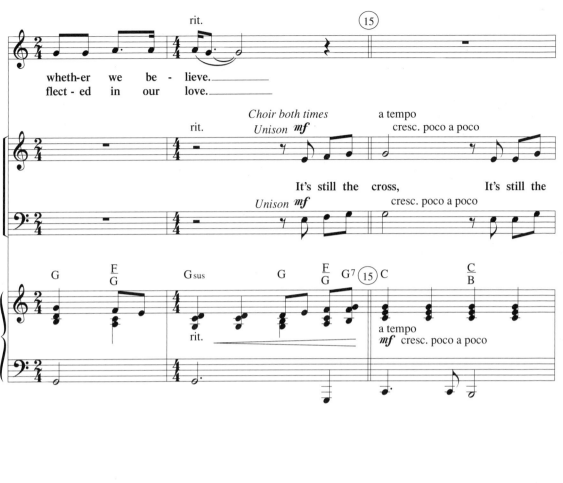

sets the cap - tive free. It's still the name, The name of

Je - sus that has pow'r to save the lost. It's still the

cross.

2. We can

name, The name of Je - sus that has pow'r to save the

lost. It's still the

lost. It's still the

They Took Him Down

by Jimmy Owens

Narrator:

They took Him down, His poor dead body,
     and prepared Him for His burial.

They took Him down, *(music begins)* His poor pale body
     drained of life, ashen, and stained
     with its own life-blood.

His healing hands, now pierced and still;
     Serving hands, that broke five loaves
     to feed five thousand;
     Holy hands, often folded in fervent prayer;
     Poor gentle hands, now pierced and still.

His poor torn feet, now bloodied and cold;
     Feet that walked weary miles
     to bring good news to broken hearts;
     Feet once washed in penitent's tears;
     Poor torn feet, now bloodied and cold.

His kingly head, made for a crown,
     now crowned– with thorns,
     His poor kingly head, crowned with thorns.

His gentle breast, now pierced
     by a spear-thrust, quiet and still;
     His poor loving breast.

His piercing eyes, now dark and blind;
     Eyes of compassion, warming the soul;
     Fiery eyes, burning at sin;
     Tender eyes, beckoning sinners;
     His piercing eyes, now dark and blind.

His matchless voice, fountain of the Father's thoughts
     stopped–
     and stilled– to speak no more.
     Silence now, where once had flowed
     Wisdom and comfort, Spirit and life;
     His matchless voice; stilled, to speak no more.

They took Him down, His poor dead body,
     and prepared Him for His burial.

Wounded Lamb

Underscore

CAMP KIRKLAND

My Redeemer Lives

My Redeemer Lives
Jesus Has Risen

Arr. by Camp Kirkland

CHOIR *"My Redeemer Lives" (Cross)
Ladies unison

Mar-y came at ear-ly dawn,

But she found her Sav-ior gone. Two in white un-

48

I know my Re - deem - er lives. I know my Re -

deem - er lives.

*"Jesus Has Risen" (Wilkinson)

ENSEMBLE
Ladies unison *mf*

54

Je - sus lay in a bor - rowed tomb for three

hand. He locked death a - way in e - ter - ni - ty's

pri - son. The grave has been con - quered for ev - er - y

man. That

Men unison

CD: 22

32

33

34

Lamb of Glory

Lamb of Glory

Lamb of Glory

Lamb of Glory

Lamb of Glory

Lamb of Glory

Lamb of Glory

Lamb of Glory

Lamb of Glory

Lamb of Glory
Lamb of Glory
Lamb of Glory
Lamb of Glory
Lamb of Glory
Lamb of Glory
Lamb of Glory
Lamb of Glory